Copyright © 2023 by Herman Strange (Author)

All rights reserved. This book or any portion thereof may not be reproduced or used in any manner whatsoever without the express written permission of the publisher except for the use of brief quotations in a book review.

This book is copyright protected. This is only for personal use. You cannot amend, distributor, sell, use, quote or paraphrase any part or the content within this book without the consent of the author. Please note the information contained within this document is for educational and entertainment purposes only. Every attempt has been made to provide accurate, up to date and reliable complete information. No warranties of any kind are expressed or implied.

Readers acknowledge that the author is not engaging in the rendering of legal, financial, medical or professional advice. The content of this book has been derived from various sources. Please consult a licensed professional before attempting any techniques outlined in this book.

By reading this document, the readers agree that under no circumstances are the author responsible for any losses, direct or indirect, which are incurred as a result of the use of information contained within this document, including but not limited to errors, omissions or inaccuracies.

Thank you very much for reading this book.

Title: Beyond the Ledger-Exploring the Revolutionary Technology Reshaping Our World
Subtitle: Understanding the Power and Potential of Blockchain for Industries and Society

Author: Herman Strange

Table of Contents

Introduction 7
  Overview of Blockchain and Its Importance 7
  The potential for blockchain to reshape industries and society 9
  The Purpose of the Book and What Readers Can Expect. 11
  An invitation for readers to engage with the material and share their thoughts and experiences 14

Chapter 1: The origins of blockchain 17
  The concept of a decentralized ledger and its development in the late 1990s 17
  The evolution of cryptographic hash functions and digital signatures 20
  The influence of previous digital currencies and ledgers on blockchain's development 23
  The release of the Bitcoin whitepaper and the creation of the first blockchain 26

Chapter 2: The early days of Bitcoin 28
  The development of the Bitcoin network and its early users 28
  The use of Bitcoin for early transactions and its early value 30
  The challenges and controversies that surrounded the early days of Bitcoin 32

    The role of early adopters and enthusiasts in the development of Bitcoin and blockchain 34

Chapter 3: The rise of altcoins and blockchain use cases 37

    The emergence of other cryptocurrencies and blockchain use cases 37

    The introduction of smart contract functionality with Ethereum 39

    The potential for blockchain in supply chain management, healthcare, and other industries 42

    The controversies and challenges that arose as blockchain gained popularity 44

Chapter 4: The evolution of blockchain technology 46

    The development of second-generation blockchains, such as EOS and TRON 46

    The role of consensus algorithms in blockchain's evolution 48

    Advances in blockchain performance, scalability, and security 50

    The potential for future blockchain innovations and advancements 54

Chapter 5: The adoption of blockchain by mainstream businesses and institutions 59

The integration of blockchain in finance, healthcare, and supply chain management 59

The benefits and challenges of blockchain adoption in mainstream industries 63

The role of regulations and standards in the adoption of blockchain 67

The potential for blockchain to revolutionize how businesses and institutions operate 71

Chapter 6: The impact of blockchain on society and the future of blockchain 74

The potential for blockchain to reshape trust, identity, and value 74

The ethical and social implications of blockchain's adoption 81

Future applications of blockchain, including in emerging technologies such as artificial intelligence and the Internet of Things 84

The challenges and opportunities that lie ahead as blockchain continues to evolve 89

Conclusion 92

The significance of blockchain in our modern world and its potential for the future 92

A summary of the book's main points and themes 95

The invitation to readers to consider their own potential involvement in the blockchain ecosystem 98
Final thoughts on the future of blockchain and its potential to impact society 100
Potential References **103**

Introduction

Overview of Blockchain and Its Importance

Blockchain is a revolutionary technology that has the potential to transform the way we exchange value and interact with each other. At its core, blockchain is a decentralized, transparent, and immutable ledger that enables trust between parties without the need for intermediaries. By eliminating the need for a trusted third party, blockchain has the potential to reduce costs, increase efficiency, and enhance security.

The decentralized nature of blockchain means that it is not controlled by any single entity, but rather by a network of users who participate in the verification and validation of transactions. This makes blockchain a more secure and tamper-proof way to record data, as it would require a majority of the network to collude in order to modify or falsify any transaction data.

The transparency of blockchain is another key feature that makes it an attractive technology for a variety of use cases. Because every transaction is recorded and visible to all participants on the network, it is difficult for any one party to manipulate the data or misrepresent the facts. This transparency can be particularly valuable in industries where trust and accountability are essential, such as finance, supply chain management, and healthcare.

Perhaps the most significant impact of blockchain, however, is its potential to reshape how we think about trust and value. Traditionally, trust has been mediated by intermediaries, such as banks, governments, and other institutions. These intermediaries provide a level of security and trust that enables us to conduct transactions, but they also come with costs and limitations. By removing intermediaries and creating a decentralized network of trust, blockchain has the potential to increase access to financial services and create new models for exchanging value.

Blockchain has already shown tremendous potential in a number of use cases, from cryptocurrency to supply chain management, healthcare, and beyond. As we continue to explore the possibilities of blockchain, it is clear that this technology will have a profound impact on our society and our economy in the years to come.

The potential for blockchain to reshape industries and society

Blockchain is a technology that has the potential to transform a wide range of industries, from finance and supply chain management to healthcare and beyond. By creating a decentralized, transparent, and secure network of trust, blockchain has the potential to increase efficiency, reduce costs, and create new business models.

In the financial industry, blockchain has already made significant strides with the emergence of cryptocurrency. Cryptocurrency is a form of digital currency that uses blockchain technology to enable secure, fast, and low-cost transactions without the need for intermediaries such as banks. With cryptocurrency, individuals can transfer value directly to one another without relying on traditional financial institutions. This has the potential to increase financial inclusion and create new business models that challenge the traditional banking industry.

Supply chain management is another industry that is ripe for disruption by blockchain technology. By using blockchain to track goods as they move through the supply chain, companies can create a transparent and tamper-proof record of each transaction, reducing the risk of fraud and increasing efficiency. This can have a significant impact on industries such as food and pharmaceuticals, where traceability and accountability are essential.

Healthcare is another industry that could benefit from blockchain technology. By using blockchain to securely store and share patient data, healthcare providers can create a more efficient and transparent system for managing patient information. This can improve patient outcomes by enabling better collaboration between healthcare providers and reducing the risk of errors and miscommunication.

Beyond specific industries, blockchain has the potential to reshape society as a whole. By creating a decentralized network of trust, blockchain has the potential to increase access to financial services, reduce corruption, and empower individuals to take control of their own data. This can lead to greater financial inclusion and a more democratic society in which individuals have greater control over their own lives.

As with any new technology, blockchain is not without its challenges and limitations. However, its potential to reshape industries and society is clear. As we continue to explore the possibilities of blockchain, it is important to consider the ethical and societal implications of this technology and work to ensure that it is used in a responsible and equitable way.

The Purpose of the Book and What Readers Can Expect

The purpose of this book is to provide readers with a comprehensive and accessible overview of blockchain technology, its history, development, and its potential to transform industries and society. The book will explore the key features of blockchain, including its decentralized nature, transparency, and security, as well as its potential to reshape industries and society.

The book will be divided into seven chapters, each focusing on a different aspect of blockchain technology. The first chapter will provide an overview of blockchain and its importance, exploring the core features that make it a revolutionary technology. The second chapter will explore the history of blockchain, from its early development to its current state, and the key milestones that have shaped its evolution.

The third chapter will explore the various types of blockchain, including public, private, and hybrid blockchains, and the different use cases for each type. The fourth chapter will focus on the technical aspects of blockchain, including consensus algorithms, smart contracts, and other key components that make blockchain possible.

The fifth chapter will explore the impact of blockchain on various industries, including finance, supply chain management, healthcare, and more. The sixth chapter will explore the potential ethical and societal implications of blockchain, including issues such as privacy, security, and decentralization.

Finally, the seventh chapter will provide a vision for the future of blockchain and its potential to transform industries and society. This chapter will explore the challenges and limitations that must be addressed in order for blockchain to reach its full potential, as well as the opportunities and possibilities that lie ahead.

Throughout the book, readers can expect to gain a comprehensive understanding of blockchain technology and its potential impact on various industries and society as a whole. The book is designed to be accessible to readers with a range of backgrounds and experience levels, from beginners to experts. Whether you are interested in the technical aspects of blockchain or its potential impact on society, this book has something to offer.

In addition to exploring the key concepts and milestones of blockchain, the book will also provide real-world examples and case studies to illustrate the practical applications of blockchain in various industries. The book will be a valuable resource for anyone looking to understand this revolutionary technology and its potential to transform our world.

An invitation for readers to engage with the material and share their thoughts and experiences

One of the core values of blockchain technology is its community-driven nature. From its early days, blockchain has been a collaborative effort, with developers, entrepreneurs, and enthusiasts from around the world working together to develop and refine this technology. It is this spirit of collaboration and innovation that has made blockchain such a revolutionary technology, and it is this same spirit that we hope to foster in this book.

We believe that the best way to understand and appreciate the potential of blockchain is to engage with the material and share our thoughts and experiences. This book is not only a resource for learning about blockchain but also a platform for sharing ideas and experiences with others.

Throughout the book, we encourage readers to engage with the material, ask questions, and share their thoughts and experiences. We believe that the collective intelligence of our readers can help us all gain a deeper understanding of this technology and its potential.

One way we will foster this community-driven approach is by incorporating real-world case studies and examples throughout the book. We will explore how blockchain technology has been applied in various industries, and how it has transformed the way we think about finance, supply chain management, healthcare, and more. We will also provide practical guidance on how readers can get involved with blockchain, whether by developing their own applications, investing in blockchain-based projects, or simply becoming more informed about this technology.

We also invite readers to share their own experiences with blockchain. If you have worked on a blockchain project, invested in a blockchain-based startup, or have ideas about how blockchain could be applied in your industry, we want to hear from you. We believe that by sharing our experiences and ideas, we can all gain a deeper understanding of the potential of blockchain technology.

Finally, we encourage readers to connect with each other through online forums, social media, and other channels. By connecting with others who share your interest in blockchain, you can gain new perspectives and insights, and collaborate on projects and ideas.

In summary, we believe that the true potential of blockchain technology can only be realized through collaboration and community. We invite readers to engage with the material, share their thoughts and experiences, and connect with others who share their interest in this revolutionary technology. Together, we can help shape the future of blockchain and its impact on industries and society.

Chapter 1: The origins of blockchain
The concept of a decentralized ledger and its development in the late 1990s

Blockchain technology may have only emerged in the past decade, but the concept of a decentralized ledger has been around since the late 1990s. At the time, a group of cryptographers and computer scientists were exploring ways to create a secure digital currency that could operate without the need for a central authority. They believed that the lack of trust in centralized financial institutions would lead to the development of alternative financial systems.

This led to the creation of several early forms of digital currencies, such as E-gold and B-Money, which relied on a decentralized ledger system to keep track of transactions. The idea behind these systems was to create a network of users who would collectively validate transactions, eliminating the need for a central authority to do so.

One of the earliest examples of this concept was Nick Szabo's proposal for "Bit Gold" in 1998, which outlined a decentralized digital currency that used a proof-of-work system to validate transactions. However, Bit Gold never gained traction, and the concept was largely forgotten until the emergence of Bitcoin a decade later.

In 2008, an unknown individual or group of individuals operating under the pseudonym Satoshi Nakamoto published a paper outlining the concept of a decentralized digital currency called Bitcoin. The paper, titled "Bitcoin: A Peer-to-Peer Electronic Cash System," described a system that relied on a decentralized ledger known as the blockchain to keep track of transactions. The blockchain would be maintained by a network of users, with each user contributing computing power to validate and process transactions.

The concept of the blockchain was critical to the success of Bitcoin, as it allowed for a decentralized system that could operate without the need for a central authority. Instead, the blockchain provided a secure, tamper-proof ledger that could be trusted by all users on the network.

The blockchain works by creating a series of blocks, with each block containing a set of validated transactions. Once a block has been validated and added to the blockchain, it becomes a permanent part of the ledger and cannot be modified. This creates a transparent, immutable ledger that can be trusted by all users on the network.

Since the emergence of Bitcoin, the concept of the blockchain has been applied to a wide range of use cases, from finance and supply chain management to healthcare and social media. The ability to create a secure, decentralized ledger that can be trusted by all users on a network has the potential to revolutionize the way we think about data management and exchange.

In summary, the concept of a decentralized ledger has been around since the late 1990s, with early forms of digital currencies like E-gold and B-Money exploring the idea of a network of users collectively validating transactions. The emergence of Bitcoin in 2008 marked the beginning of the blockchain era, with the blockchain providing a secure, decentralized ledger that could be trusted by all users on the network. Since then, the concept of the blockchain has been applied to a wide range of use cases, with the potential to reshape industries and society.

The evolution of cryptographic hash functions and digital signatures

Blockchain technology relies on a variety of cryptographic tools to provide secure, decentralized ledgers that can be trusted by all users on a network. Two of the most critical of these tools are cryptographic hash functions and digital signatures.

A cryptographic hash function is a mathematical algorithm that takes an input (such as a file or message) and produces a fixed-size output (known as a hash or digest) that represents the original input. The hash function is designed to be a one-way function, meaning it is very difficult (if not impossible) to recreate the original input from the hash output.

Cryptographic hash functions have been around for decades, with early examples dating back to the 1970s. Over time, these functions have evolved to become more complex and secure, with modern hash functions like SHA-256 and SHA-3 providing high levels of security and collision resistance.

Digital signatures, on the other hand, are a way to provide proof of authenticity and integrity for digital documents or messages. A digital signature is created by applying a mathematical algorithm to a message, producing a unique signature that can be verified by anyone who has the public key associated with the signer.

Digital signatures have also been around for decades, with early examples dating back to the 1980s. However, these early systems were often complicated and cumbersome to use, requiring specialized hardware and software to generate and verify signatures.

The evolution of cryptographic hash functions and digital signatures has played a critical role in the development of blockchain technology. The blockchain relies on a variety of cryptographic tools to provide a secure, decentralized ledger that can be trusted by all users on the network.

In the case of the blockchain, cryptographic hash functions are used to create a fixed-size digital fingerprint (known as a hash) of each block in the chain. Each block includes the hash of the previous block in the chain, creating a tamper-proof record of all transactions on the network.

Digital signatures are used to ensure that only the owner of a particular wallet can authorize transactions from that wallet. When a user creates a transaction, they use their private key to sign the transaction, creating a unique digital signature that can be verified by anyone on the network who has access to the user's public key.

Together, these cryptographic tools provide a powerful set of tools for creating secure, decentralized ledgers that can be trusted by all users on a network. The evolution of cryptographic hash functions and digital signatures has played a critical role in the development of the blockchain, and these tools will continue to be important as the blockchain continues to evolve and find new applications.

In summary, cryptographic hash functions and digital signatures are critical components of blockchain technology, providing the tools necessary to create secure, decentralized ledgers that can be trusted by all users on a network. The evolution of these tools has played a critical role in the development of the blockchain, and they will continue to be important as the blockchain continues to find new applications.

The influence of previous digital currencies and ledgers on blockchain's development

While blockchain technology is often seen as a revolutionary development, it is important to recognize that it has been influenced by a variety of previous digital currencies and ledgers. In this section, we will explore some of the key historical precedents that paved the way for the development of the blockchain.

One of the earliest examples of a digital currency was eCash, which was developed in the early 1990s by David Chaum. eCash used blind signatures to provide a way to transfer digital money without revealing the identity of the sender or the recipient. While eCash ultimately failed to gain widespread adoption, it laid the groundwork for the development of later digital currencies.

Another early example of a digital currency was B-Money, which was proposed by Wei Dai in 1998. B-Money was designed to be a decentralized digital currency that would allow users to make anonymous transactions without the need for a centralized authority. While B-Money was never implemented, it influenced the development of later digital currencies like Bitcoin.

In 2008, Satoshi Nakamoto published a paper that proposed a new digital currency called Bitcoin. Bitcoin was designed to be a decentralized digital currency that would allow users to make peer-to-peer transactions without the need for a centralized authority. Bitcoin's key innovation was the blockchain, a decentralized ledger that provided a way to record transactions in a tamper-proof and transparent way.

The blockchain was not the first decentralized ledger, however. In the early 2000s, a number of decentralized systems were developed, including BitTorrent and Freenet. These systems used decentralized architectures to provide a way to share files without the need for a centralized server. The development of these systems paved the way for the development of the blockchain, which applied the same principles to create a decentralized ledger for financial transactions.

One of the key features of the blockchain is its ability to provide transparency and accountability in a decentralized system. This idea can be traced back to the concept of triple entry accounting, which was proposed by Yuji Ijiri in 1989. Triple entry accounting provides a way to create a tamper-proof record of financial transactions, with each transaction recorded in three places: in the debit and credit accounts, as well as in a third, decentralized ledger.

The development of previous digital currencies and ledgers played a critical role in the development of the blockchain. These systems laid the groundwork for the idea of decentralized systems, which ultimately led to the development of the blockchain. The blockchain's key innovation was the creation of a decentralized ledger that could be trusted by all users on the network, providing a way to create a tamper-proof and transparent record of financial transactions.

In summary, the development of previous digital currencies and ledgers played a critical role in the development of the blockchain. These systems laid the groundwork for the idea of decentralized systems, which ultimately led to the development of the blockchain. The blockchain's key innovation was the creation of a decentralized ledger that could be trusted by all users on the network, providing a way to create a tamper-proof and transparent record of financial transactions.

The release of the Bitcoin whitepaper and the creation of the first blockchain

"The release of the Bitcoin whitepaper and the creation of the first blockchain" marks a critical turning point in the development of blockchain technology. This subtopic explores the circumstances surrounding the creation of the first blockchain, beginning with the release of the Bitcoin whitepaper by the pseudonymous Satoshi Nakamoto in 2008.

The subtopic will delve into the key features of the Bitcoin whitepaper, including its focus on solving the problem of double-spending in digital currencies, its proposed solution through the creation of a decentralized ledger, and its use of cryptographic proof of work to secure the network.

Furthermore, this subtopic will examine the initial development of the Bitcoin blockchain, from its first block being mined by Satoshi Nakamoto on January 3, 2009, to the growth of the network and its early adopters. It will also explore the challenges and criticisms the early blockchain faced, including its association with illicit activities and its lack of scalability.

The subtopic will highlight the significance of the Bitcoin whitepaper and the creation of the first blockchain in the context of blockchain's development as a whole. It will discuss how this event paved the way for the emergence of other blockchain-based projects, including other digital currencies, smart contract platforms, and more.

Overall, this subtopic will provide readers with a detailed understanding of the origins of blockchain and how the creation of the first blockchain has shaped the development of this technology.

Chapter 2: The early days of Bitcoin
The development of the Bitcoin network and its early users

"The development of the Bitcoin network and its early users" marks the beginning of the practical application of blockchain technology. This subtopic explores the early days of the Bitcoin network, starting from its initial release in 2009 to its growth and adoption in the years that followed.

This subtopic will discuss the technical advancements made to the Bitcoin protocol, such as the implementation of the first software updates and the establishment of the Bitcoin Foundation. It will also highlight the role of early adopters in the development and promotion of the Bitcoin network, including their involvement in mining, trading, and promoting the use of the digital currency.

Furthermore, this subtopic will explore the challenges faced by the early Bitcoin network, including regulatory hurdles and security concerns. It will also delve into the growth of the Bitcoin ecosystem, including the creation of the first Bitcoin exchanges and merchant adoption.

The subtopic will also touch on some of the notable events and controversies surrounding the early days of Bitcoin, such as the first Bitcoin pizza purchase, the shutdown of the Silk Road, and the Mt. Gox exchange collapse.

Overall, this subtopic provides readers with an in-depth understanding of the early days of Bitcoin and the development of the network. It offers insights into the technical, social, and economic factors that contributed to the growth of the Bitcoin ecosystem, and how it set the stage for the emergence of other blockchain-based projects.

The use of Bitcoin for early transactions and its early value

"The use of Bitcoin for early transactions and its early value" is a subtopic in chapter 2 that explores the emergence of Bitcoin as a new form of digital currency and its initial value. This subtopic provides readers with a comprehensive understanding of how Bitcoin was first used as a medium of exchange and how its value emerged.

In this subtopic, readers will be introduced to the first Bitcoin transactions that took place in the early days of the network. This will include the purchase of a pizza in exchange for 10,000 BTC, the first-known transaction using Bitcoin as a medium of exchange. This subtopic will also highlight other early transactions, such as the purchase of goods on online marketplaces and the use of Bitcoin for donations to various charities.

The subtopic will also discuss the factors that contributed to the initial value of Bitcoin. This will include an analysis of how the first Bitcoin exchange, Mt. Gox, emerged and how it allowed for the trading of Bitcoin against other currencies, such as the US dollar. Readers will learn about how the value of Bitcoin was initially determined, and how its value evolved over time.

In addition, this subtopic will explore the challenges that the early Bitcoin ecosystem faced in terms of adoption, including the general lack of awareness of the currency, the complexity of its use, and its early association with illicit activities. It will discuss how the early users of Bitcoin addressed these challenges and how the cryptocurrency gained its early adoption.

This subtopic will also touch on the impact of early adopters, including those who mined Bitcoin in its early days and established it as a new form of currency. It will highlight the community of early users and developers who were instrumental in laying the groundwork for Bitcoin's success.

Overall, this subtopic will provide readers with a comprehensive understanding of the early use of Bitcoin for transactions, how its value emerged, and the challenges that the network faced in its early days. It will also highlight the important role that early adopters played in establishing the Bitcoin network and promoting its adoption as a new form of currency.

The challenges and controversies that surrounded the early days of Bitcoin

In its early days, Bitcoin faced a number of challenges and controversies that threatened to derail its development and adoption. Some of the key issues and controversies during this period include:

1. The Silk Road: The Silk Road was an online marketplace that operated on the dark web, selling illegal drugs and other illicit items. Bitcoin was the preferred payment method on the Silk Road, leading to concerns that the currency was being used for criminal activities.

2. Mt. Gox: Mt. Gox was one of the first and largest Bitcoin exchanges, but it eventually filed for bankruptcy in 2014 after losing hundreds of millions of dollars worth of Bitcoin. The incident raised questions about the security and stability of Bitcoin exchanges, and whether they could be trusted to hold and manage large amounts of cryptocurrency.

3. Regulatory challenges: In the early days of Bitcoin, there was a lack of clarity around how the currency should be regulated. Governments around the world struggled to determine how to classify Bitcoin and how to deal with its unique characteristics, such as its decentralized nature and its potential for anonymous transactions.

4. Volatility: Like many new financial assets, Bitcoin was subject to extreme volatility in its early days. The currency's value could swing wildly in a matter of hours or days, making it difficult for businesses and investors to rely on it as a stable store of value.

5. Technical challenges: In addition to these more high-profile challenges, there were a number of technical challenges facing the Bitcoin network in its early days. These included issues around scalability, security, and the potential for fraud and double-spending.

Despite these challenges, however, the early years of Bitcoin also saw the emergence of a dedicated community of users and developers who were committed to overcoming these obstacles and realizing the potential of the technology. In many ways, it was these early challenges and controversies that helped to shape the Bitcoin ecosystem and set the stage for its ongoing development and adoption.

The role of early adopters and enthusiasts in the development of Bitcoin and blockchain

The development of Bitcoin and blockchain technology was largely driven by a passionate community of early adopters and enthusiasts. These individuals saw the potential for a decentralized currency and network that could challenge the traditional financial system and promote a more democratic and transparent way of conducting transactions.

One of the key figures in the early Bitcoin community was Satoshi Nakamoto, the anonymous creator of Bitcoin. Nakamoto's identity remains a mystery, but his vision for a decentralized currency and network has had a profound impact on the world.

In addition to Nakamoto, there were many other early adopters and enthusiasts who played a significant role in the development of Bitcoin and blockchain technology. These individuals were driven by a desire to promote a more democratic and decentralized way of conducting transactions, and they worked tirelessly to develop the technology and build the network.

One of the ways that early adopters and enthusiasts contributed to the development of Bitcoin was through the creation of mining pools. These pools allowed individual miners to combine their computing power and increase their chances of earning Bitcoin rewards. This helped to make the mining process more accessible and efficient, which in turn helped to support the growth of the network.

Early adopters and enthusiasts also contributed to the development of the Bitcoin software and infrastructure. They created tools and services that made it easier for people to use and transact with Bitcoin, and they worked to promote the technology and educate others about its potential benefits.

However, there were also challenges and controversies that surrounded the early days of Bitcoin and blockchain technology. One of the biggest challenges was the perception that Bitcoin was primarily used for illegal activities, such as money laundering and drug trafficking. This perception created a stigma around Bitcoin and made it difficult for the technology to gain mainstream acceptance.

Another challenge was the fact that early versions of the Bitcoin software were not very user-friendly, which made it difficult for people without technical expertise to use and transact with Bitcoin. This limited the growth of the network and made it difficult for the technology to gain widespread adoption.

Despite these challenges, early adopters and enthusiasts remained committed to the development of Bitcoin and blockchain technology. They continued to work on improving the technology and promoting its potential benefits, and their efforts ultimately helped to pave the way for the widespread adoption of blockchain technology that we see today.

Chapter 3: The rise of altcoins and blockchain use cases

The emergence of other cryptocurrencies and blockchain use cases

As the concept of blockchain began to gain popularity, other cryptocurrencies began to emerge in the market. In this chapter, we will explore the rise of altcoins and other blockchain use cases.

One of the first major altcoins to gain prominence was Litecoin, which was launched in 2011. Litecoin was created as a faster and more efficient alternative to Bitcoin, with faster block generation times and lower transaction fees. Other altcoins soon followed, each with their own unique features and use cases.

One notable example is Ethereum, which introduced the concept of smart contracts to the blockchain. Smart contracts are self-executing contracts with the terms of the agreement written directly into code, allowing for decentralized applications to be built on top of the blockchain.

Other cryptocurrencies and blockchain use cases include Ripple, which is designed for cross-border payments and transactions, and Dash, which offers increased privacy and anonymity features. There are also blockchain projects focused on areas such as identity management, supply chain management, and data storage.

In addition to altcoins, blockchain technology has been applied in various industries beyond finance. For example, the healthcare industry has explored the use of blockchain for securely storing and sharing patient medical records, while the energy industry has looked into using blockchain for more efficient energy trading and tracking.

As the potential of blockchain technology continues to be explored, we can expect to see more altcoins and blockchain use cases emerging in the future.

The introduction of smart contract functionality with Ethereum

The introduction of smart contract functionality with Ethereum marked a major milestone in the evolution of blockchain technology. While Bitcoin was designed primarily as a peer-to-peer electronic cash system, Ethereum was created to enable the development of decentralized applications (dApps) and smart contracts, which are self-executing digital contracts with the terms of the agreement written directly into code.

Ethereum was first proposed in 2013 by Vitalik Buterin, a young programmer from Toronto, Canada. Buterin's idea was to create a blockchain platform that would be more flexible and versatile than Bitcoin, allowing developers to create a wide range of decentralized applications. In 2014, Buterin published the Ethereum whitepaper, which laid out the technical details of the new platform.

The key innovation behind Ethereum was the introduction of a new programming language called Solidity, which allows developers to write smart contracts that can be executed on the Ethereum Virtual Machine (EVM). The EVM is a decentralized, Turing-complete virtual machine that can run any code written in Solidity, making it possible to create complex dApps that can automate a wide range of processes.

The first version of the Ethereum software was released in July 2015, and the platform quickly gained popularity among developers and entrepreneurs. One of the first major dApps to be built on Ethereum was Augur, a decentralized prediction market that allows users to bet on the outcome of real-world events. Other early dApps included Golem, a decentralized supercomputer, and MakerDAO, a decentralized lending platform.

Since then, the Ethereum ecosystem has continued to grow, with thousands of developers building and launching new dApps on the platform. Some of the most notable examples include Uniswap, a decentralized exchange for trading cryptocurrencies, Aave, a decentralized lending and borrowing platform, and CryptoKitties, a blockchain-based game that allows users to breed and trade digital cats.

The introduction of smart contract functionality with Ethereum opened up a whole new world of possibilities for blockchain technology. With the ability to automate complex processes and create new decentralized applications, blockchain technology became much more than just a tool for digital currency. Today, Ethereum and other smart contract platforms are at the forefront of the blockchain revolution, powering a wide range of innovative new products and services that have the potential to transform the way we live and work.

The potential for blockchain in supply chain management, healthcare, and other industries

Blockchain technology has the potential to transform various industries beyond the financial sector. One of the most promising areas is supply chain management, which can benefit from the transparency, security, and efficiency that blockchain provides.

Supply chain management involves various stages, including sourcing, manufacturing, distribution, and retailing. Traditionally, supply chains are fragmented, with different parties using their own systems, leading to silos of information that make it difficult to track and manage products.

Blockchain technology can help overcome these challenges by creating a shared, immutable ledger that enables all participants to access and update information in real-time. This can help streamline processes, reduce costs, and increase efficiency.

One of the most well-known examples of blockchain in supply chain management is IBM's Food Trust Network, which is designed to enhance transparency and traceability in the food supply chain. By using blockchain, food companies can track food items from farm to table, ensuring that they are safe and high-quality.

In addition to supply chain management, blockchain also holds potential in healthcare, where it can improve data sharing and security. Blockchain can help patients have more control over their data, enabling them to share their health records with doctors and researchers while maintaining privacy and security.

Another potential application of blockchain is in identity management, where it can help individuals store and share their personal data securely and conveniently. Blockchain-based identity solutions could help reduce identity theft and fraud while giving people more control over their personal data.

Overall, the potential use cases for blockchain technology are vast and varied, and many industries are exploring how they can benefit from this technology. As blockchain continues to evolve and mature, we can expect to see even more use cases and applications in the years to come.

The controversies and challenges that arose as blockchain gained popularity

As blockchain technology gained more attention and adoption, it also faced challenges and controversies. In this section, we will explore some of the key controversies and challenges that arose as blockchain gained popularity.

1. Scalability: One of the major challenges that blockchain faces is scalability. With the increasing number of transactions on the blockchain, it becomes increasingly difficult to process them all in a timely manner. As a result, some blockchain networks have faced long transaction confirmation times and high fees, making it difficult to use them for everyday transactions.

2. Security and privacy: While blockchain is often lauded for its security, there have been several high-profile hacks and thefts of cryptocurrencies. Additionally, the transparent nature of the blockchain means that users' transactions and identities are publicly visible, which can pose a challenge for privacy-conscious individuals and organizations.

3. Regulation: The decentralized and global nature of blockchain has made it challenging for regulators to establish clear guidelines and regulations around its use. This has led to a patchwork of regulations around the world, with some

countries embracing blockchain and others taking a more cautious approach.

4. Energy consumption: The process of validating transactions on a blockchain network, known as mining, requires significant amounts of computational power and energy. This has led to concerns about the environmental impact of blockchain, particularly as the popularity of cryptocurrencies continues to grow.

5. Adoption challenges: While the potential for blockchain to transform various industries is significant, there are still challenges to its widespread adoption. These include technical challenges, such as the need for more user-friendly interfaces and development tools, as well as social and cultural challenges, such as the need for more education and awareness around blockchain's potential benefits.

Overall, the controversies and challenges that have arisen around blockchain highlight the need for ongoing research and development to address these issues and ensure that blockchain can reach its full potential as a transformative technology.

Chapter 4: The evolution of blockchain technology
The development of second-generation blockchains, such as EOS and TRON

The early days of blockchain technology were dominated by Bitcoin, but as the potential of blockchain became more apparent, other projects began to emerge. Second-generation blockchains, also known as smart contract platforms, sought to improve on the limitations of Bitcoin's blockchain and enable more advanced functionality.

One of the earliest second-generation blockchains to gain attention was Ethereum. Launched in 2015, Ethereum introduced the concept of smart contracts, which enabled developers to create and deploy decentralized applications (Dapps) on top of the blockchain. By using a programming language called Solidity, developers could create complex logic and automate the execution of transactions, opening up a wide range of new use cases for blockchain technology.

Since then, several other second-generation blockchains have emerged, each with their own unique features and capabilities. For example, EOS and TRON are two prominent examples of blockchains that aim to enable high-performance, scalable Dapps. EOS uses a delegated proof-of-stake (DPoS) consensus mechanism that allows for fast transaction processing and high throughput, while TRON focuses on enabling decentralized content distribution and social media platforms.

Other second-generation blockchains have taken different approaches, such as Cardano's focus on academic research and formal verification, or Polkadot's goal of enabling interoperability between different blockchains. These projects have continued to evolve and improve, with new features and upgrades being added over time.

Overall, the development of second-generation blockchains has been a key part of the evolution of blockchain technology. By enabling more advanced functionality and use cases, these blockchains have opened up new possibilities for decentralized applications and helped to spur innovation in the industry.

The role of consensus algorithms in blockchain's evolution

Consensus algorithms are at the heart of blockchain technology. They are the mechanisms that allow for the agreement and validation of transactions on a decentralized network. As blockchain technology has evolved, so too have the consensus algorithms that power it.

One of the earliest and most well-known consensus algorithms is Proof-of-Work (PoW), which is used by Bitcoin and other early cryptocurrencies. PoW requires users to perform complex calculations in order to validate transactions, and rewards them with newly minted tokens for doing so. While effective in its early days, PoW has been criticized for its high energy consumption and slow transaction processing times.

As a result, many newer blockchains have developed alternative consensus algorithms that aim to address these issues. One such algorithm is Proof-of-Stake (PoS), which requires users to "stake" their tokens in order to validate transactions. This allows for a more energy-efficient process, as it does not require the intensive calculations of PoW.

Other consensus algorithms include Delegated Proof-of-Stake (DPoS), which allows users to delegate their staking power to "witnesses" who validate transactions on their behalf, and Byzantine Fault Tolerance (BFT), which allows for fast transaction processing and high fault tolerance.

The evolution of consensus algorithms has allowed for greater efficiency, scalability, and security in blockchain technology. It has also opened up new possibilities for applications and use cases, as well as new challenges for developers and users to overcome. As the technology continues to evolve, it is likely that new consensus algorithms will continue to emerge and shape the future of blockchain.

Advances in blockchain performance, scalability, and security

Advances in blockchain performance, scalability, and security have been a critical part of the technology's evolution since its inception. As blockchain technology has become more mainstream and the number of users and transactions has grown, scalability and performance have become increasingly important.

One of the main challenges that blockchain technology has faced is the limited number of transactions that can be processed in a given time period. Bitcoin, for example, can only process around seven transactions per second, while Visa can process up to 24,000 transactions per second. This has led to long wait times and high transaction fees, which have made blockchain less appealing for certain applications.

To address these challenges, there have been several advances in blockchain technology that have improved performance and scalability. One of the most significant advances has been the development of new consensus algorithms that allow for faster and more efficient transaction processing.

One such algorithm is the delegated proof-of-stake (DPoS) algorithm, which is used by blockchains such as EOS and TRON. With DPoS, token holders elect a limited number of delegates who are responsible for validating transactions and adding them to the blockchain. This system is faster and more energy-efficient than the proof-of-work (PoW) algorithm used by Bitcoin and other early blockchains, which requires significant computational resources to solve complex mathematical problems.

Other consensus algorithms that have been developed to improve blockchain performance include proof-of-stake (PoS), proof-of-authority (PoA), and practical Byzantine fault tolerance (pBFT). Each of these algorithms has its own unique features and benefits, and they are being used in various blockchains for different applications.

In addition to advances in consensus algorithms, there have been developments in blockchain architecture that have improved performance and scalability. For example, sharding is a technique that divides the blockchain into smaller, more manageable pieces called shards. This allows for parallel processing of transactions, which can significantly increase the number of transactions that can be processed in a given time period.

Another important development in blockchain architecture is the use of off-chain solutions such as state channels and sidechains. These solutions allow for certain transactions to occur off the main blockchain, reducing the overall load on the network and increasing scalability.

Along with performance and scalability, security has also been a major area of focus for blockchain technology. One of the key features of blockchain is its immutability, which means that once a transaction is recorded on the blockchain, it cannot be altered or deleted. This feature is critical for ensuring the integrity of the blockchain, but it also presents challenges when it comes to security.

To address these challenges, there have been developments in blockchain security that have improved the technology's ability to withstand attacks and prevent fraud. For example, multi-signature technology allows for more secure control of transactions by requiring multiple parties to sign off on a transaction before it can be processed.

Another important security feature that has been developed is zero-knowledge proofs, which allow for the verification of a transaction without revealing any information about the transaction itself. This can help protect sensitive information and ensure privacy on the blockchain.

Overall, the evolution of blockchain technology has been driven by the need to address performance, scalability, and security challenges. Through advances in consensus algorithms, blockchain architecture, and security features, the technology has continued to improve and expand its potential applications.

The potential for future blockchain innovations and advancements

As blockchain technology continues to evolve and expand, it's exciting to consider the potential for future innovations and advancements. Here are some of the most promising areas for future blockchain development.

a. Interoperability

One of the biggest challenges facing blockchain technology is its lack of interoperability. Currently, most blockchain networks are siloed, meaning they can't easily communicate with each other. However, efforts are underway to create solutions that would enable different blockchain networks to work together seamlessly. One potential solution is the use of "bridges" or "relay" chains that act as intermediaries between different blockchains. Another potential solution is the development of "interoperability protocols" that enable different blockchains to communicate with each other directly.

b. Scalability

Another challenge facing blockchain technology is scalability. Most blockchain networks are limited in terms of the number of transactions they can handle per second. However, there are several promising solutions being developed to address this issue. One approach is the use of sharding, which involves breaking a blockchain network into smaller pieces, each of which can handle its own set of transactions. Another approach is the use of off-chain solutions, such as sidechains or state channels, that enable transactions to be processed off the main blockchain, thereby reducing the load on the main network.

c. Privacy

Another area of blockchain innovation is privacy. While the public nature of most blockchain networks provides transparency and security, it also means that all transactions are visible to anyone with access to the network. However, there are several approaches to enhancing privacy in blockchain transactions, including the use of zero-knowledge proofs, ring signatures, and homomorphic encryption.

d. Energy efficiency

The energy consumption required for mining and maintaining most blockchain networks has been a point of criticism for some time. However, there are promising developments in this area as well. One approach is the use of alternative consensus algorithms that require less energy than proof of work, such as proof of stake or proof of authority. Another approach is the use of renewable energy sources to power blockchain networks.

e. Decentralized finance (DeFi)

Decentralized finance, or DeFi, is an area of blockchain innovation that has exploded in popularity in recent years. DeFi refers to financial applications built on blockchain networks that operate independently of traditional financial institutions. Examples of DeFi applications include decentralized exchanges, lending platforms, and stablecoins. As DeFi continues to grow and evolve, it has the potential to disrupt traditional financial systems and provide greater access to financial services for people around the world.

f. Digital identity

Digital identity is another area of blockchain innovation that has the potential to transform the way we manage and protect our personal information. By using blockchain technology to create a decentralized and tamper-proof system for storing and verifying identity information, individuals could have greater control over their personal data and be better protected against identity theft and fraud.

g. Supply chain management

Blockchain technology also has the potential to transform supply chain management. By creating a tamper-proof and transparent ledger of all transactions along a supply chain, blockchain could provide greater transparency and accountability, reduce the risk of fraud and counterfeiting, and help to ensure ethical and sustainable practices throughout the supply chain.

h. Social impact

Finally, blockchain technology has the potential to drive social impact in a variety of areas. For example, blockchain could be used to create transparent and secure systems for distributing aid and resources to people in need, or to create decentralized systems for voting and governance that are resistant to corruption and manipulation.

*****

In conclusion, the potential for future blockchain innovations and advancements is virtually limitless. The technology has already shown significant promise in transforming industries such as finance, supply chain management, and healthcare, and new use cases are continually emerging. As second-generation blockchains continue to develop, we can expect to see improvements in scalability, security, and interoperability, which will open up even more possibilities for blockchain applications.

Beyond these improvements, we can also expect to see the emergence of new consensus algorithms and governance models, which could further enhance blockchain's performance and security. There is also significant potential for blockchain to be combined with other emerging technologies, such as artificial intelligence, the internet of things, and decentralized finance, to create even more powerful solutions.

Of course, there are also challenges to be overcome. For example, blockchain's complexity can make it difficult for non-technical users to fully understand and utilize the technology. Additionally, as blockchain adoption increases, there may be challenges related to regulation and governance, as governments and institutions seek to balance the benefits of blockchain with concerns over security and privacy.

Overall, however, the future of blockchain looks bright. With continued innovation and collaboration between developers, entrepreneurs, and institutions, we can expect to see even more impactful blockchain applications in the years to come. The technology has the potential to revolutionize the way we do business, govern our societies, and interact with one another, and it will be exciting to see how this potential is realized in the coming years.

Chapter 5: The adoption of blockchain by mainstream businesses and institutions

The integration of blockchain in finance, healthcare, and supply chain management

The integration of blockchain technology in various industries is an exciting development that could bring about significant changes in how businesses and institutions operate. From finance to healthcare to supply chain management, the potential applications of blockchain are vast and varied.

Finance

One of the most promising applications of blockchain technology is in the field of finance. Blockchain's ability to provide a secure and transparent ledger could have a significant impact on financial institutions, which have traditionally relied on centralized intermediaries to facilitate transactions. By using blockchain technology, financial institutions can streamline their processes and reduce the cost of doing business while providing a more secure and transparent experience for their customers.

One area where blockchain is already making an impact is in cross-border payments. Companies such as Ripple are leveraging blockchain technology to provide faster, cheaper, and more secure cross-border payments than traditional systems. The use of blockchain in the financial industry is not limited to cross-border payments, however. Blockchain technology can also be used for asset management, securities trading, and even the issuance of digital currencies.

Healthcare

Another industry that stands to benefit from blockchain technology is healthcare. With patient data being one of the most sensitive types of information, the use of blockchain technology can help ensure the secure sharing and management of health information. Blockchain can also be used to track the supply chain of drugs and medical devices, ensuring that they are not counterfeit or tampered with.

Blockchain technology can also help improve the research and development of new drugs. Clinical trials require vast amounts of data, which can be difficult to manage and analyze. Blockchain can provide a secure and transparent way to manage this data, allowing researchers to draw meaningful insights and conclusions.

Supply Chain Management

Supply chain management is another area where blockchain technology is being increasingly adopted. By using blockchain, companies can track products throughout the supply chain, from raw materials to the end product. This not only provides transparency but also allows for greater efficiency, as companies can identify and address issues in the supply chain more quickly.

Blockchain technology can also be used to ensure the authenticity and provenance of products, such as luxury goods or high-end wines. By using blockchain, consumers can be confident that they are purchasing a genuine product, which can help combat counterfeiting and fraud.

Challenges and Limitations

While the adoption of blockchain technology in various industries is exciting, there are still some challenges and limitations that need to be addressed. One of the biggest challenges is the lack of standardization in the blockchain industry. With so many different blockchain platforms and protocols, it can be challenging for businesses and institutions to choose the right solution for their needs.

Another challenge is the issue of scalability. As more and more businesses and institutions adopt blockchain technology, there will be a need for increased capacity and performance. While blockchain technology has made significant advances in this area, there is still work to be done to ensure that blockchain can handle the demands of large-scale applications.

Finally, there is the issue of regulation. As blockchain technology becomes more mainstream, there will be a need for clear and consistent regulation to ensure that the technology is used ethically and responsibly. While some countries have already implemented regulations around blockchain and cryptocurrencies, others are still in the process of doing so.

Conclusion

The adoption of blockchain technology by mainstream businesses and institutions is an exciting development that could bring about significant changes in various industries. From finance to healthcare to supply chain management, blockchain has the potential to provide increased efficiency, transparency, and security. However, there are still challenges and limitations that need to be addressed before blockchain can reach its full potential. With continued innovation and collaboration, the future of blockchain looks bright.

The benefits and challenges of blockchain adoption in mainstream industries

The adoption of blockchain by mainstream businesses and institutions has been on the rise in recent years. From finance to healthcare to supply chain management, many industries are exploring the potential of blockchain technology to streamline processes, increase efficiency, and improve security. While the benefits of blockchain adoption are clear, there are also significant challenges that must be addressed to fully realize its potential.

Benefits of Blockchain Adoption in Mainstream Industries

One of the primary benefits of blockchain adoption in mainstream industries is increased efficiency. Blockchain can reduce the need for intermediaries and automate processes that previously required manual intervention. In supply chain management, for example, blockchain can track products from their origin to their final destination, reducing the need for manual record-keeping and paperwork. This can reduce errors and delays, as well as help to prevent fraud and counterfeiting.

Another benefit of blockchain adoption is increased transparency. In finance, for example, blockchain can be used to improve transparency and reduce the risk of fraud.

Transactions can be tracked in real-time, providing greater visibility into financial activity. This can help to increase trust between financial institutions and their customers, as well as reduce the risk of financial crime.

Blockchain can also improve security in mainstream industries. By providing a decentralized and tamper-proof ledger, blockchain can help to protect sensitive information from unauthorized access or modification. This is particularly important in healthcare, where sensitive patient information must be protected from data breaches and cyber attacks.

Challenges of Blockchain Adoption in Mainstream Industries

While the benefits of blockchain adoption in mainstream industries are significant, there are also significant challenges that must be addressed to fully realize its potential.

One of the primary challenges is the lack of regulatory clarity. Many industries are subject to strict regulations, and the use of blockchain technology can raise questions about compliance. For example, in finance, the use of blockchain may require the development of new regulatory frameworks to ensure compliance with anti-money laundering (AML) and know your customer (KYC) regulations.

Another challenge is the need for interoperability between different blockchain platforms. As more industries adopt blockchain, there is a risk of fragmentation, with different platforms using different standards and protocols. This can make it difficult to share data and collaborate across different industries.

Scalability is also a significant challenge for blockchain adoption in mainstream industries. While blockchain is well-suited for small-scale applications, it can struggle to handle large-scale transactions. This is particularly problematic in finance, where high transaction volumes are the norm.

Finally, there is a need for education and awareness about blockchain technology. Many businesses and institutions may not fully understand the potential of blockchain, or may be hesitant to adopt new technologies due to a lack of familiarity. There is a need for education and training programs to help businesses and institutions understand the benefits of blockchain and how to effectively integrate it into their operations.

Conclusion

The adoption of blockchain by mainstream businesses and institutions is an important step in the evolution of blockchain technology. While the benefits of blockchain adoption are clear, there are also significant challenges that must be addressed to fully realize its potential. These include regulatory clarity, interoperability, scalability, and education and awareness. By addressing these challenges, we can create a more secure, transparent, and efficient future for a wide range of industries.

The role of regulations and standards in the adoption of blockchain

The adoption of blockchain technology by mainstream businesses and institutions has been increasing rapidly in recent years. As more and more companies are exploring the potential of blockchain in various industries, the role of regulations and standards is becoming increasingly important. In this chapter, we will explore the role of regulations and standards in the adoption of blockchain and their impact on the development of the technology.

Regulations and Standards in Blockchain

Blockchain technology is still relatively new, and the regulatory framework surrounding it is still evolving. There are a few different areas of regulation that impact blockchain, including financial regulations, data protection laws, and securities laws.

In the financial industry, many countries have implemented regulations to oversee the use of cryptocurrencies and other blockchain-based financial products. For example, the U.S. Securities and Exchange Commission (SEC) has been actively monitoring the use of Initial Coin Offerings (ICOs), and has taken legal action against companies that it believes have violated securities laws. In addition, the Financial Action Task Force (FATF), an intergovernmental organization that sets standards for anti-money laundering (AML) and counter-terrorism financing (CTF), has issued guidance on how cryptocurrencies and other blockchain-based financial products should be regulated.

Data protection laws are also relevant to blockchain technology, as blockchain systems often involve the processing of personal data. The European Union's General Data Protection Regulation (GDPR) requires companies to obtain explicit consent from individuals before collecting and processing their personal data. In addition, the regulation requires companies to ensure that individuals can exercise their rights to access, correct, and delete their personal data.

Beyond data protection laws, various regulatory bodies around the world have started taking a closer look at blockchain and its potential implications. For example, in the United States, the Securities and Exchange Commission (SEC) has been monitoring the cryptocurrency and blockchain space, particularly with regards to initial coin offerings (ICOs). In July 2017, the SEC published a report that concluded that certain ICOs may be considered securities and therefore subject to federal securities laws. This has led to increased scrutiny and regulation in the ICO space.

Similarly, in the European Union, the European Securities and Markets Authority (ESMA) has published guidance on the regulatory implications of blockchain, particularly with regards to securities regulation. In addition, the European Commission has been exploring the potential regulatory implications of blockchain, particularly in the areas of financial services and data protection.

Regulations and standards are also important for blockchain adoption in other industries, such as supply chain management. The use of blockchain in supply chain management has the potential to increase transparency, reduce fraud, and improve efficiency. However, the adoption of blockchain in this space requires adherence to existing industry standards and regulations. For example, the food industry has various regulations in place to ensure the safety and quality of food products. Blockchain solutions in this space must comply with these regulations in order to be effective.

Moreover, standards are also critical to the adoption of blockchain. Standards can help ensure interoperability and compatibility between different blockchain systems, as well as provide guidelines for the development of secure and reliable blockchain solutions. The International Organization for Standardization (ISO) has established a technical committee to develop standards for blockchain and distributed ledger technologies. This committee is currently working on developing standards related to blockchain interoperability, smart contracts, and security.

In conclusion, the role of regulations and standards in the adoption of blockchain cannot be overstated. As blockchain technology continues to evolve and mature, it is important for regulatory bodies and industry stakeholders to work together to develop appropriate standards and regulations that will facilitate the adoption of blockchain in a responsible and sustainable way. By doing so, we can harness the potential of blockchain to transform industries and improve the lives of people around the world.

The potential for blockchain to revolutionize how businesses and institutions operate

Blockchain technology has the potential to revolutionize how businesses and institutions operate in a wide range of industries. This potential is largely due to the unique features of blockchain technology, including decentralization, immutability, transparency, and security.

One of the most significant potential benefits of blockchain technology is its ability to streamline and automate business processes. By using smart contracts and blockchain-based platforms, businesses can reduce the time and cost associated with manual processes, such as contract management, record-keeping, and payment processing. For example, blockchain technology can be used to create automated supply chain management systems that track products from raw materials to finished goods, reducing the time and cost associated with manual record-keeping and reducing the risk of fraud or errors.

Another potential benefit of blockchain technology is its ability to enhance transparency and accountability. By providing a decentralized and immutable record of transactions, blockchain technology can help businesses and institutions to increase trust and accountability in their operations. For example, blockchain-based platforms can be used to create transparent and auditable systems for voting, charity donations, and government spending, reducing the risk of corruption and increasing public trust.

Blockchain technology can also help to enhance data security and privacy. The use of cryptographic algorithms and distributed ledgers can provide a high degree of protection against cyberattacks and data breaches. In addition, blockchain technology can be used to create secure and private systems for data sharing and storage, allowing businesses and institutions to maintain control over their data while still facilitating secure data sharing.

However, despite the potential benefits of blockchain technology, there are also challenges and limitations that must be addressed before widespread adoption can occur. One of the biggest challenges is scalability, as current blockchain systems can be slow and inefficient when processing large volumes of data. Another challenge is interoperability, as different blockchain platforms and systems may not be compatible with each other.

In addition, there are concerns around the energy consumption associated with blockchain mining, which requires significant computing power and energy usage. This has led to the development of more energy-efficient consensus algorithms and the exploration of alternative energy sources, such as renewable energy.

Regulatory challenges also exist, particularly as blockchain technology can operate in a decentralized and borderless environment. Governments and regulatory bodies are still grappling with how to regulate blockchain technology, including issues such as data protection, anti-money laundering, and tax compliance.

Despite these challenges, the potential for blockchain technology to revolutionize how businesses and institutions operate is significant. As the technology continues to evolve and mature, it is likely that we will see increased adoption of blockchain-based solutions in a wide range of industries.

Chapter 6: The impact of blockchain on society and the future of blockchain

The potential for blockchain to reshape trust, identity, and value

Blockchain technology has the potential to reshape how trust, identity, and value are established and managed. These three concepts are closely interrelated, and the emergence of blockchain has the potential to revolutionize how they are perceived and utilized. In this section, we will explore the potential for blockchain to reshape trust, identity, and value, and its implications for society.

Reshaping Trust

Trust is the foundation of all social, economic, and political interactions. In the traditional world, trust is often established through intermediaries such as banks, governments, and other trusted third parties. These intermediaries act as gatekeepers of trust, managing and verifying transactions, identities, and contracts. However, intermediaries are expensive, time-consuming, and often prone to corruption, errors, and fraud.

Blockchain has the potential to replace intermediaries with decentralized networks that enable trust to be established and maintained without the need for trusted third parties. By using cryptographic algorithms and consensus mechanisms, blockchain can enable trust to be established and maintained through a distributed network of nodes. This means that transactions can be verified and recorded by a network of participants, without the need for a central authority. This has the potential to reduce costs, increase efficiency, and enhance transparency and accountability.

The potential for blockchain to reshape trust can be seen in the rise of decentralized finance (DeFi) applications. DeFi is a rapidly growing area of blockchain that enables financial transactions to be conducted without the need for banks or other intermediaries. DeFi applications are built on top of blockchain platforms and use smart contracts to automate financial transactions such as lending, borrowing, and trading. This has the potential to democratize finance and make it more accessible to a broader range of people, particularly those who are unbanked or underbanked.

Reshaping Identity

Identity is another critical concept that blockchain has the potential to reshape. In the traditional world, identity is established and managed through centralized databases managed by governments and other trusted third parties. These databases often contain sensitive personal information, and their management is often prone to errors, breaches, and abuse.

Blockchain can enable identity to be established and managed in a decentralized and secure manner. By using cryptographic algorithms and consensus mechanisms, blockchain can enable individuals to control and manage their identities without the need for centralized authorities. This means that individuals can control who has access to their personal information and how it is used.

The potential for blockchain to reshape identity can be seen in the rise of decentralized identity (DID) solutions. DID is a rapidly growing area of blockchain that enables individuals to create and control their digital identities. DID solutions use blockchain to create secure and tamper-proof identity records that are managed by the individual. This has the potential to enable individuals to manage their identities more effectively and reduce the risk of identity theft and fraud.

Reshaping Value

Value is a fundamental concept that underpins all economic transactions. In the traditional world, value is often established and managed through centralized financial systems such as banks, stock markets, and other intermediaries. These systems often have high fees, limited accessibility, and are often prone to manipulation and fraud.

Blockchain has the potential to enable value to be established and managed in a decentralized and transparent manner. By using cryptographic algorithms and consensus mechanisms, blockchain can enable value to be transferred and recorded without the need for centralized authorities. This means that transactions can be conducted more quickly, cheaply, and transparently.

The potential for blockchain to reshape value can be seen in the rise of blockchain-based marketplaces and platforms. These platforms enable value to be exchanged without the need for intermediaries such as banks, governments, and other trusted third parties. This has the potential to reduce costs, increase transparency, and enhance trust between buyers and sellers.

Implications for Society

The potential for blockchain to reshape trust, identity, and value has significant implications for society. One of the key implications is the potential for blockchain to create new models of trust. Blockchain technology has the potential to enable trust to be established in a decentralized and distributed manner, without the need for intermediaries. This could have significant implications for areas such as e-commerce, where intermediaries such as payment processors and escrow services play a significant role in establishing trust between buyers and sellers.

In addition, blockchain technology could have a profound impact on the way that identity is established and managed. Blockchain-based identity solutions could provide a secure and tamper-proof way of establishing and verifying identity, which could have applications in areas such as banking, healthcare, and voting systems. This could have a significant impact on reducing fraud and increasing security.

Another area where blockchain could have significant implications is in the way that value is created and exchanged. With the rise of digital assets and cryptocurrencies, blockchain technology has created new models for the creation and exchange of value. This could have significant implications for the way that we think about money and financial systems, and could even lead to the creation of entirely new models for economic organization.

Challenges and Limitations

Despite the potential of blockchain to reshape trust, identity, and value, there are also significant challenges and limitations that must be addressed. One of the key challenges is scalability. Many blockchain systems are limited in the number of transactions they can process per second, which could limit their potential for widespread adoption in areas such as e-commerce and financial systems.

In addition, there are challenges around privacy and data protection. While blockchain systems are designed to be secure and tamper-proof, this can also make it difficult to remove data once it has been recorded on the blockchain. This could create challenges around compliance with data protection laws, such as the GDPR.

Another challenge is the complexity of blockchain technology. Blockchain systems can be difficult to understand and use, which could limit their adoption by businesses and individuals who do not have a technical background. This could limit the potential for blockchain to reshape trust, identity, and value in areas such as e-commerce and financial systems.

The Future of Blockchain

Despite these challenges, the potential for blockchain to reshape trust, identity, and value is significant, and there is a growing interest in the technology from businesses, governments, and individuals. As the technology continues to evolve and mature, it is likely that we will see new applications and use cases emerge, which could have a profound impact on the way that we live, work, and interact with one another.

One area where we are already seeing significant growth is in the use of blockchain-based digital assets and cryptocurrencies. These have created new models for the creation and exchange of value, and could have significant implications for the way that we think about money and financial systems.

Another area where we are likely to see significant growth is in the development of blockchain-based identity solutions. These could provide a secure and tamper-proof way of establishing and verifying identity, which could have applications in areas such as banking, healthcare, and voting systems.

Overall, the potential for blockchain to reshape trust, identity, and value is significant, and the technology is likely to play an increasingly important role in our lives in the years to come. While there are challenges and limitations that must be addressed, the future of blockchain is bright, and it is an exciting time to be involved in the development and adoption of this transformative technology.

The ethical and social implications of blockchain's adoption

The adoption of blockchain technology has the potential to bring about significant benefits to society, but it also raises ethical and social implications that need to be addressed. This subtopic will explore the ethical and social implications of blockchain's adoption, including issues related to privacy, security, accessibility, and inequality.

Privacy and Security

One of the primary ethical implications of blockchain technology is related to privacy and security. Blockchain's decentralization and immutability make it an attractive option for secure data storage, but this same feature can also make it difficult for individuals to control their personal information. Once information is stored on the blockchain, it cannot be erased or altered, which can pose a significant risk to an individual's privacy. As a result, there is a need to develop privacy-enhancing technologies that enable users to control their data and to ensure that blockchain systems are designed with privacy in mind.

Accessibility

Another ethical implication of blockchain's adoption is related to accessibility. While blockchain technology has the potential to bring about significant benefits, it can also be difficult for some individuals to access and use. For example, individuals who do not have access to the internet or who lack the necessary technical skills may find it challenging to participate in blockchain networks. This lack of accessibility can exacerbate existing inequalities and create new ones.

Inequality

Blockchain's adoption can also have significant social implications related to inequality. While blockchain technology has the potential to create new opportunities and improve access to financial services, it can also reinforce existing power structures and inequalities. For example, individuals or organizations with more resources may be better able to participate in blockchain networks and benefit from the technology's advantages, while those with fewer resources may be left behind.

Regulatory and Legal Frameworks

The adoption of blockchain technology also raises significant regulatory and legal challenges. As blockchain networks become more integrated into society, there is a need to develop regulatory and legal frameworks that can ensure the technology is used in a safe and responsible manner. This includes developing guidelines and standards for blockchain development, establishing clear rules for data protection, and addressing issues related to the use of smart contracts.

Environmental Impact

The environmental impact of blockchain's adoption is another important ethical implication that needs to be considered. Blockchain networks consume a significant amount of energy, which can contribute to climate change. As blockchain networks become more popular, there is a need to develop sustainable solutions that minimize the environmental impact of the technology.

Conclusion

The ethical and social implications of blockchain's adoption are complex and multifaceted. While the technology has the potential to bring about significant benefits to society, it also poses significant risks and challenges that need to be addressed. To ensure that blockchain is used in a safe, responsible, and ethical manner, it is essential to develop clear guidelines and standards, and to ensure that the technology is designed with privacy, accessibility, and sustainability in mind. By doing so, we can ensure that blockchain technology is used in a manner that benefits all members of society, rather than exacerbating existing power structures and inequalities.

Future applications of blockchain, including in emerging technologies such as artificial intelligence and the Internet of Things

As blockchain technology continues to evolve, it is increasingly being explored as a potential solution for a range of emerging technologies. Two areas where blockchain could have a significant impact in the future are artificial intelligence (AI) and the Internet of Things (IoT).

AI is the development of computer systems that can perform tasks that typically require human intelligence, such as visual perception, speech recognition, decision-making, and language translation. AI has the potential to revolutionize many industries, but it requires large amounts of data to train the algorithms that power these systems. This data is often siloed in different organizations and is difficult to access and share. Blockchain technology could provide a solution to this problem by creating a decentralized, secure, and transparent platform for sharing data.

One potential application of blockchain and AI is in the field of healthcare. Medical data is highly sensitive and is often siloed within individual healthcare providers or institutions. However, to develop effective AI algorithms for medical diagnosis and treatment, large amounts of data from different sources are needed. By using blockchain to securely and transparently share medical data, AI systems could be trained on a much larger dataset, potentially leading to more accurate diagnoses and treatments.

Another area where blockchain and AI could be used together is in the development of autonomous vehicles. These vehicles require vast amounts of data to operate safely, such as traffic patterns, weather conditions, and road infrastructure. Blockchain technology could provide a secure and transparent platform for sharing this data between vehicles and infrastructure, enabling real-time updates and enhancing safety.

The Internet of Things (IoT) is another emerging technology that could benefit from the use of blockchain. The IoT refers to the network of physical devices, vehicles, home appliances, and other items embedded with electronics, software, sensors, and connectivity, which allows these objects to connect and exchange data. With the rise of the IoT, the need for secure and efficient data sharing has become increasingly important. Blockchain technology could provide a secure and transparent platform for IoT devices to share data with each other, enabling the development of new applications and services.

One potential application of blockchain and IoT is in the development of smart cities. Smart cities are urban areas that use IoT devices and sensors to collect and analyze data, with the goal of improving efficiency, sustainability, and quality of life. Blockchain technology could provide a secure and transparent platform for these devices to share data, enabling real-time monitoring and analysis of city systems such as traffic, energy, and waste management.

Another area where blockchain and IoT could be used together is in supply chain management. The IoT can be used to track the movement of goods and products throughout the supply chain, but this data is often siloed within individual organizations. By using blockchain to securely and transparently share data, supply chain participants could gain greater visibility into the movement of goods, leading to improved efficiency, reduced costs, and enhanced transparency.

As blockchain technology continues to evolve, it is likely that new and innovative applications will be developed. By combining blockchain with emerging technologies such as AI and IoT, it is possible to create new solutions that could have a significant impact on a range of industries and sectors.

Conclusion

As emerging technologies continue to develop, it is becoming increasingly clear that blockchain will play an important role in shaping the future of technology. Blockchain has the potential to revolutionize the way that we think about trust, identity, and value, and to transform industries ranging from finance and healthcare to supply chain management and beyond.

As the technology continues to evolve, we can expect to see even more innovative applications of blockchain in areas such as artificial intelligence and the Internet of Things. By enabling secure and decentralized data storage and communication, blockchain could help to unlock the full potential of these transformative technologies, while also addressing some of the key challenges around privacy, security, and trust.

However, as with any emerging technology, there are also ethical and social implications to consider when it comes to the adoption of blockchain. As blockchain becomes more ubiquitous, it is important to ensure that it is being used in a responsible and ethical manner, and that its benefits are being shared across all members of society.

Ultimately, the future of blockchain is both exciting and uncertain, and much will depend on how the technology continues to develop and how it is adopted by businesses, institutions, and individuals around the world. However, one thing is clear: blockchain is here to stay, and it has the potential to transform the way we live, work, and interact with each other in ways that we are only beginning to imagine.

The challenges and opportunities that lie ahead as blockchain continues to evolve

As blockchain technology continues to evolve, there are numerous challenges and opportunities that lie ahead for businesses, governments, and individuals. In this section, we will examine some of the key challenges and opportunities that are likely to emerge in the coming years as blockchain technology continues to mature.

Challenges:

Scalability: One of the biggest challenges facing blockchain technology is scalability. Most existing blockchains are limited in their ability to handle large volumes of transactions. As more businesses and individuals adopt blockchain, there will be a need for more scalable blockchain solutions.

Interoperability: With the increasing number of blockchains being developed, there is a growing need for interoperability between different blockchains. This will enable businesses and individuals to seamlessly transfer assets and data across different blockchain platforms.

Regulation: As blockchain becomes more mainstream, there will be increased regulatory scrutiny. Governments around the world are already beginning to explore how to regulate blockchain-based activities, and there is likely to be more regulation in the future.

Energy consumption: One of the criticisms of blockchain is its high energy consumption. As blockchain adoption grows, there will be an increasing need for more energy-efficient solutions.

Security: Blockchain technology is generally considered to be secure, but there are still potential vulnerabilities that could be exploited by hackers. As the value of assets stored on blockchains grows, there will be an increased need for better security solutions.

Opportunities:

Decentralization: Blockchain technology enables decentralization, which means that power is distributed among many participants rather than being concentrated in the hands of a few. This has the potential to promote more open and democratic systems.

Transparency: Blockchain technology enables transparent and auditable records, which can increase trust in business and government systems. This has the potential to increase accountability and reduce corruption.

Efficiency: Blockchain technology can streamline many processes, reducing the need for intermediaries and improving efficiency. This has the potential to reduce costs and increase productivity.

Innovation: Blockchain technology enables new forms of innovation, such as the development of decentralized applications and new business models. This has the potential to create new opportunities for businesses and individuals.

New markets: As blockchain technology becomes more widely adopted, there will be new markets for blockchain-based products and services. This has the potential to create new economic opportunities.

As blockchain technology continues to evolve, it is likely that new challenges and opportunities will emerge. However, by being aware of these challenges and opportunities, businesses, governments, and individuals can position themselves to take advantage of the benefits of blockchain technology while mitigating its potential drawbacks.

Conclusion

The significance of blockchain in our modern world and its potential for the future

Blockchain technology has come a long way since its inception, and its potential applications continue to expand. Its ability to provide a secure and transparent platform for recording and verifying transactions has made it an attractive option for businesses, governments, and individuals looking for ways to improve efficiency, security, and trust in a digital world.

The rise of Bitcoin and other cryptocurrencies in recent years has brought blockchain technology into the mainstream, leading to increased interest and investment in the technology. However, blockchain's potential goes far beyond digital currencies. The decentralized nature of blockchain makes it suitable for a wide range of applications, including supply chain management, healthcare, identity management, and voting systems.

As blockchain technology continues to evolve, it will face both challenges and opportunities. The technology will need to address issues of scalability, security, and energy consumption to become a more practical solution for mainstream use. At the same time, as blockchain becomes more integrated into our lives, there will be a need for regulatory frameworks to ensure that the technology is used ethically and transparently.

Despite these challenges, the potential benefits of blockchain technology are vast. By improving transparency, trust, and security in a range of applications, blockchain has the potential to reshape the way we do business, govern, and interact with each other. It has the potential to disrupt existing systems and open up new opportunities for innovation and collaboration.

One of the key benefits of blockchain technology is its potential to democratize access to financial services. By providing a secure and transparent platform for financial transactions, blockchain can enable individuals and businesses who have historically been excluded from traditional financial systems to access banking and financial services. This could have a significant impact on poverty reduction and economic development in developing countries.

Another potential benefit of blockchain is its ability to provide secure and transparent systems for managing and sharing data. This could have significant implications for healthcare, where blockchain could provide a secure and efficient way to manage patient data and improve patient outcomes. It could also be used to improve supply chain management, where blockchain could provide greater transparency and traceability in the movement of goods and products.

As blockchain technology continues to evolve, it will also become more integrated with other emerging technologies, such as artificial intelligence and the Internet of Things. This integration could lead to new and innovative applications of blockchain, such as decentralized autonomous organizations (DAOs) and smart cities.

In conclusion, blockchain technology has the potential to revolutionize the way we do business, govern, and interact with each other. Its ability to provide secure and transparent systems for managing transactions and data has already had a significant impact on a wide range of industries, from finance to healthcare to supply chain management. As the technology continues to evolve, it will face both challenges and opportunities, but its potential benefits are vast. With the right investment, regulation, and innovation, blockchain technology could transform our modern world and shape the future of our society.

A summary of the book's main points and themes

As blockchain technology has continued to evolve and gain popularity, it has become increasingly important to understand its potential impact on our society, economy, and future. This book has explored various aspects of blockchain technology, including its history, evolution, adoption by mainstream businesses and institutions, and its potential for future innovations and applications.

Throughout this book, we have seen that blockchain has the potential to revolutionize how we trust, transact, and interact with each other. Its unique features, such as decentralization, immutability, and transparency, offer new opportunities for building trust and creating value in a wide range of applications.

One of the key themes of this book has been the role of blockchain in disrupting traditional industries and creating new business models. We have seen how blockchain is being integrated into finance, healthcare, supply chain management, and other industries, and how it is changing the way these industries operate. Blockchain has the potential to improve efficiency, reduce costs, and enhance security and transparency, which can benefit both businesses and consumers.

Another important theme of this book has been the challenges and opportunities that lie ahead as blockchain continues to evolve. While blockchain has the potential to create significant value and impact, it also faces a number of challenges, including scalability, interoperability, and regulatory issues. Addressing these challenges will require collaboration and innovation from a wide range of stakeholders, including businesses, policymakers, and technologists.

The ethical and social implications of blockchain's adoption have also been discussed in this book. As with any new technology, blockchain raises important questions about privacy, security, and trust. While blockchain has the potential to enhance privacy and security, it also creates new risks and challenges that need to be addressed. It is important to ensure that blockchain is developed and deployed in a responsible and ethical manner, with a focus on creating value for society as a whole.

Looking to the future, this book has explored the potential for blockchain to revolutionize emerging technologies such as artificial intelligence and the Internet of Things. By integrating blockchain with these technologies, we can create new opportunities for collaboration, data sharing, and trust.

In summary, this book has provided a comprehensive overview of blockchain technology and its potential impact on our society and economy. From its early beginnings as a technology for digital currencies, blockchain has evolved into a powerful tool for building trust, creating value, and disrupting traditional industries. As blockchain continues to evolve, it will be important for businesses, policymakers, and technologists to work together to address the challenges and opportunities that lie ahead, and to ensure that blockchain is developed and deployed in a responsible and ethical manner.

The invitation to readers to consider their own potential involvement in the blockchain ecosystem

As we conclude our exploration of the evolution, adoption, and impact of blockchain technology, it is worth considering the role that each of us can play in shaping the future of this revolutionary technology.

Blockchain technology is still in its infancy, and there is much work to be done to realize its full potential. As we have seen throughout this book, blockchain has the potential to transform how we conduct transactions, store and share data, and build trust and transparency in a variety of industries. From finance and healthcare to supply chain management and beyond, blockchain is poised to revolutionize the way we do business.

But for this potential to be realized, it will require the active participation of individuals and organizations across a variety of sectors. As a reader of this book, you have already taken an important first step in understanding the technology and its potential. But there is much more that you can do to get involved in the blockchain ecosystem.

For individuals, this might mean learning more about blockchain technology and the industries in which it is being applied. It might mean investing in blockchain-based projects or even building your own blockchain-based application. As the technology continues to evolve, there will be more and more opportunities for individuals to get involved and make a difference.

For organizations, the potential applications of blockchain are even more significant. Blockchain technology has the potential to transform entire industries, creating new efficiencies, lowering costs, and improving transparency and security. For businesses and institutions that are able to harness this potential, the benefits could be enormous.

However, for organizations to effectively implement blockchain technology, it will require a significant investment of time, resources, and expertise. It will require collaboration with other stakeholders, including regulators, other businesses, and technology providers. And it will require a willingness to embrace new business models and ways of working.

In conclusion, the potential for blockchain technology to transform our world is enormous. But realizing this potential will require the active participation of individuals and organizations across a variety of sectors. As we move forward, it is up to each of us to consider our own potential involvement in the blockchain ecosystem and to take action to help shape the future of this revolutionary technology.

Final thoughts on the future of blockchain and its potential to impact society

As we come to the end of this book, we have explored the various facets of blockchain technology, from its history to its potential impact on society. We have seen how blockchain has the potential to revolutionize many different industries, from finance to healthcare, and how it has the potential to reshape how we think about trust, identity, and value.

Looking ahead to the future, it is clear that blockchain technology will continue to evolve and improve, as developers work to overcome the challenges of scalability, performance, and security. As blockchain becomes more widely adopted by businesses and institutions, it will be important to establish clear regulations and standards to ensure that the technology is used responsibly and ethically.

One of the most exciting aspects of blockchain technology is its potential to create new and innovative solutions to some of the world's most pressing problems. For example, blockchain could be used to create more transparent and accountable supply chains, to facilitate cross-border payments, or to improve access to healthcare records.

As blockchain technology continues to evolve and improve, it is likely that we will see it being integrated with other emerging technologies, such as artificial intelligence and the Internet of Things. This integration has the potential to create powerful new solutions that can help us address some of the world's most complex challenges.

At the same time, it is important to acknowledge that blockchain technology is not a silver bullet that can solve all of the world's problems. As with any technology, it has its limitations and challenges, and it is important to approach it with a clear-eyed perspective.

In the end, the future of blockchain technology will depend on a wide range of factors, from the actions of individual developers and businesses to the policies of governments and international organizations. As individuals, we can all play a role in shaping the future of blockchain by staying informed about the latest developments and by considering our own potential involvement in the blockchain ecosystem.

In conclusion, blockchain technology has the potential to be one of the most significant technological developments of our time. Its ability to create transparent and accountable systems has the potential to revolutionize many different industries and to create new solutions to some of the world's most pressing problems. As we move forward, it will be important to continue exploring the potential of this technology and to work together to ensure that it is used responsibly and ethically.

THE END

Potential References

Introduction:

Narayanan, A., Bonneau, J., Felten, E., Miller, A., & Goldfeder, S. (2016). Bitcoin and Cryptocurrency Technologies: A Comprehensive Introduction. Princeton University Press.

Swan, M. (2015). Blockchain: Blueprint for a New Economy. O'Reilly Media, Inc.

Chapter 1:

Nakamoto, S. (2008). Bitcoin: A Peer-to-Peer Electronic Cash System. https://bitcoin.org/bitcoin.pdf

Narayanan, A., Bonneau, J., Felten, E., Miller, A., & Goldfeder, S. (2016). Bitcoin and Cryptocurrency Technologies: A Comprehensive Introduction. Princeton University Press.

Chapter 2:

Popper, N. (2015). Digital Gold: Bitcoin and the Inside Story of the Misfits and Millionaires Trying to Reinvent Money. Harper Collins.

Tapscott, D., & Tapscott, A. (2016). Blockchain Revolution: How the Technology Behind Bitcoin is Changing Money, Business, and the World. Penguin.

Chapter 3:

Tapscott, D., & Tapscott, A. (2016). Blockchain Revolution: How the Technology Behind Bitcoin is Changing Money, Business, and the World. Penguin.

Swan, M. (2015). Blockchain: Blueprint for a New Economy. O'Reilly Media, Inc.

Chapter 4:

Antonopoulos, A. M. (2014). Mastering Bitcoin: Unlocking Digital Cryptocurrencies. O'Reilly Media, Inc.

Tapscott, D., & Tapscott, A. (2016). Blockchain Revolution: How the Technology Behind Bitcoin is Changing Money, Business, and the World. Penguin.

Chapter 5:

Casey, M. J., & Vigna, P. (2018). The Truth Machine: The Blockchain and the Future of Everything. St. Martin's Press.

Crosby, M., Pattanayak, P., Verma, S., & Kalyanaraman, V. (2016). Blockchain Technology: Beyond Bitcoin. Applied Innovation, 2(6-10).

Chapter 6:

Casey, M. J., & Vigna, P. (2018). The Truth Machine: The Blockchain and the Future of Everything. St. Martin's Press.

Swan, M. (2015). Blockchain: Blueprint for a New Economy. O'Reilly Media, Inc.

Conclusion:

Crosby, M., Pattanayak, P., Verma, S., & Kalyanaraman, V. (2016). Blockchain Technology: Beyond Bitcoin. Applied Innovation, 2(6-10).

Tapscott, D., & Tapscott, A. (2016). Blockchain Revolution: How the Technology Behind Bitcoin is Changing Money, Business, and the World. Penguin.

www.ingramcontent.com/pod-product-compliance
Lightning Source LLC
LaVergne TN
LVHW012122070526
838202LV00056B/5826